HALLOWEEN HIDDEN PICTURES

Coloring Characters For Kids

THIS BOOK
BELONGS TO

_____

All rights reserved. No part of this publication may be reproduced, stored in retrieval system, copied in any form or by any means, electronic, mechanical, photocopying, recording or otherwise transmitted without written permission from the publisher.

Copyrighted Material

Kayry Hall

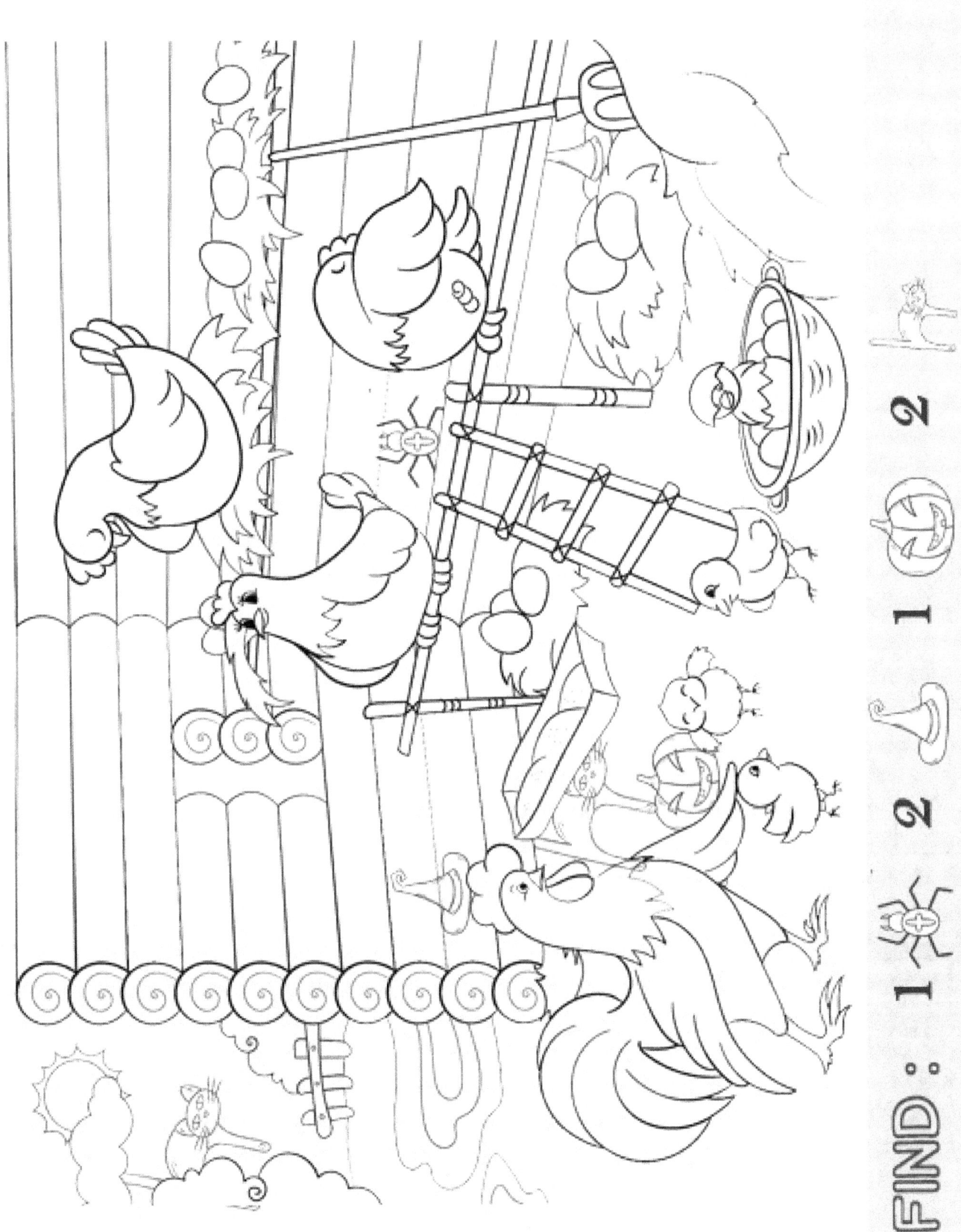

FIND: 1 🕷 2 🍄 1 🏐 2 🎃 1 🐱

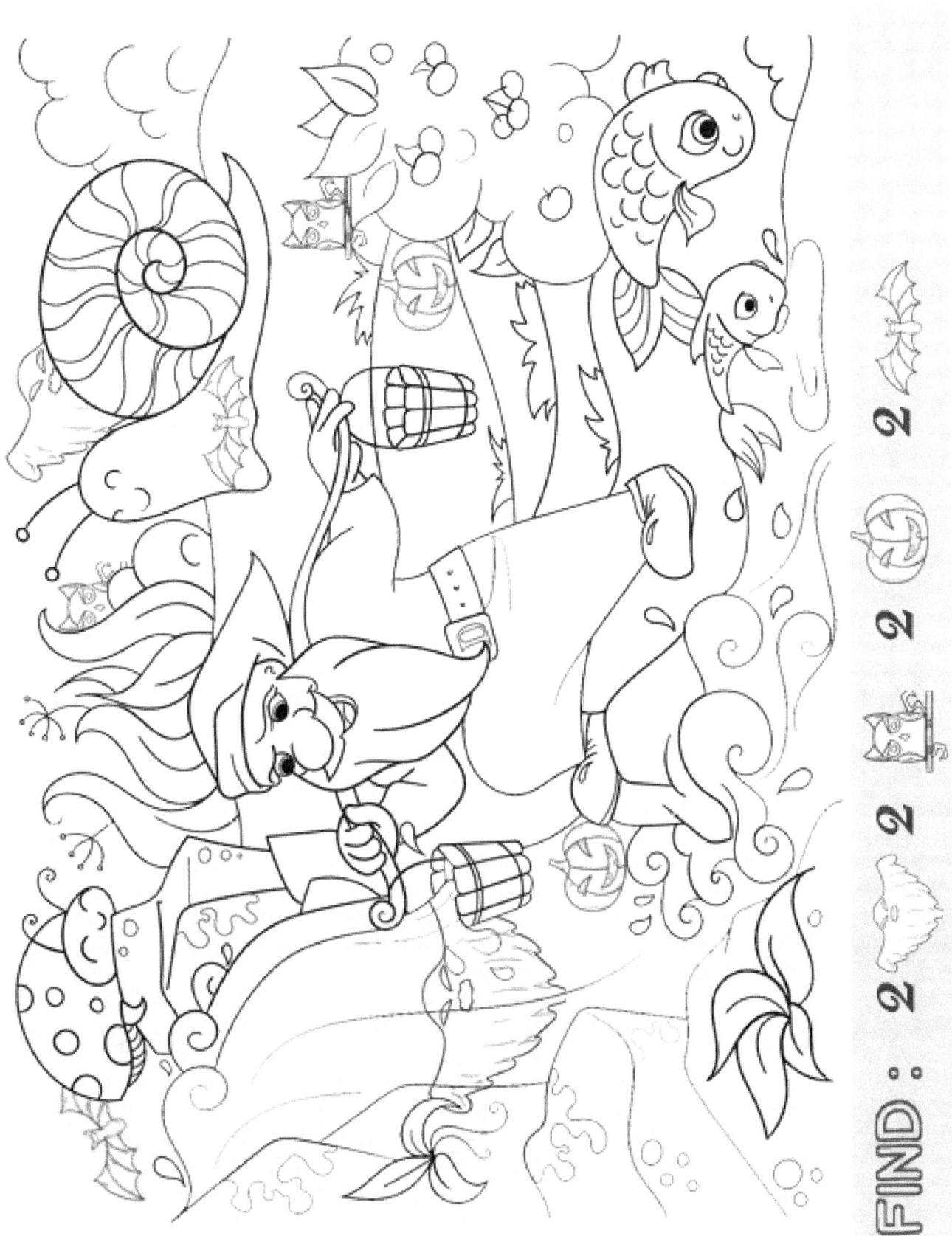

FIND: 2 🦇 2 🎃 2 🐟 2 🚩 2 🦇

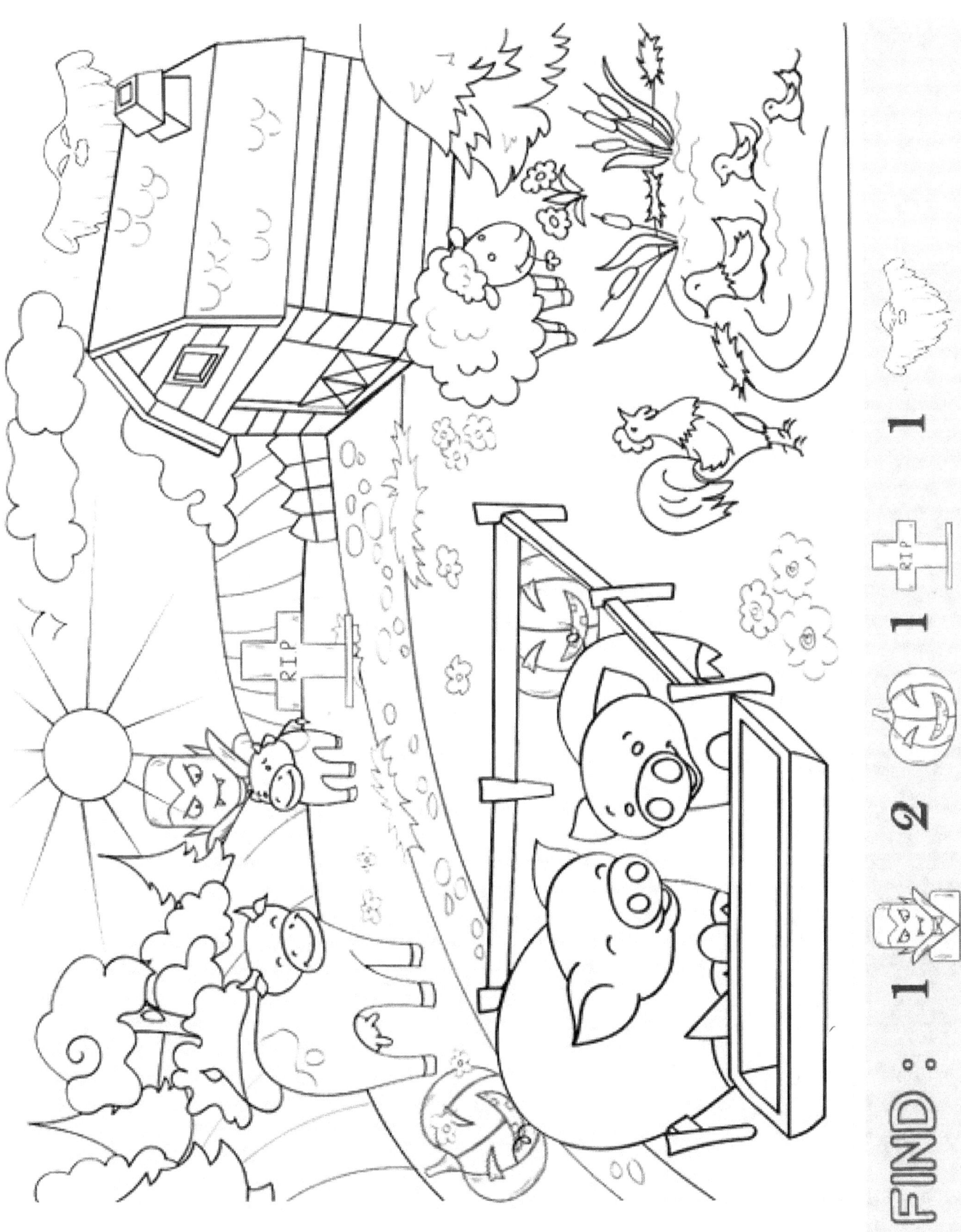

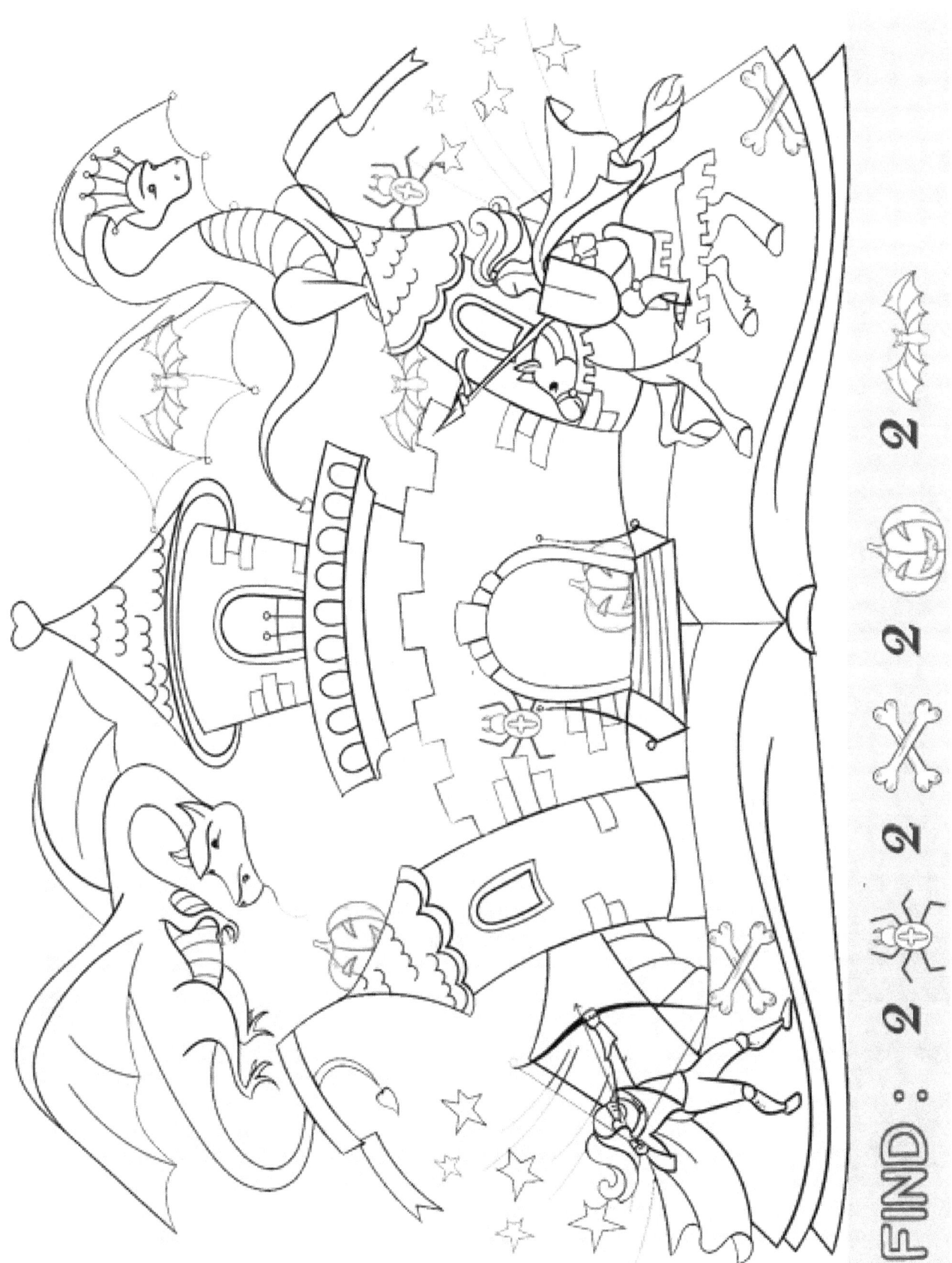

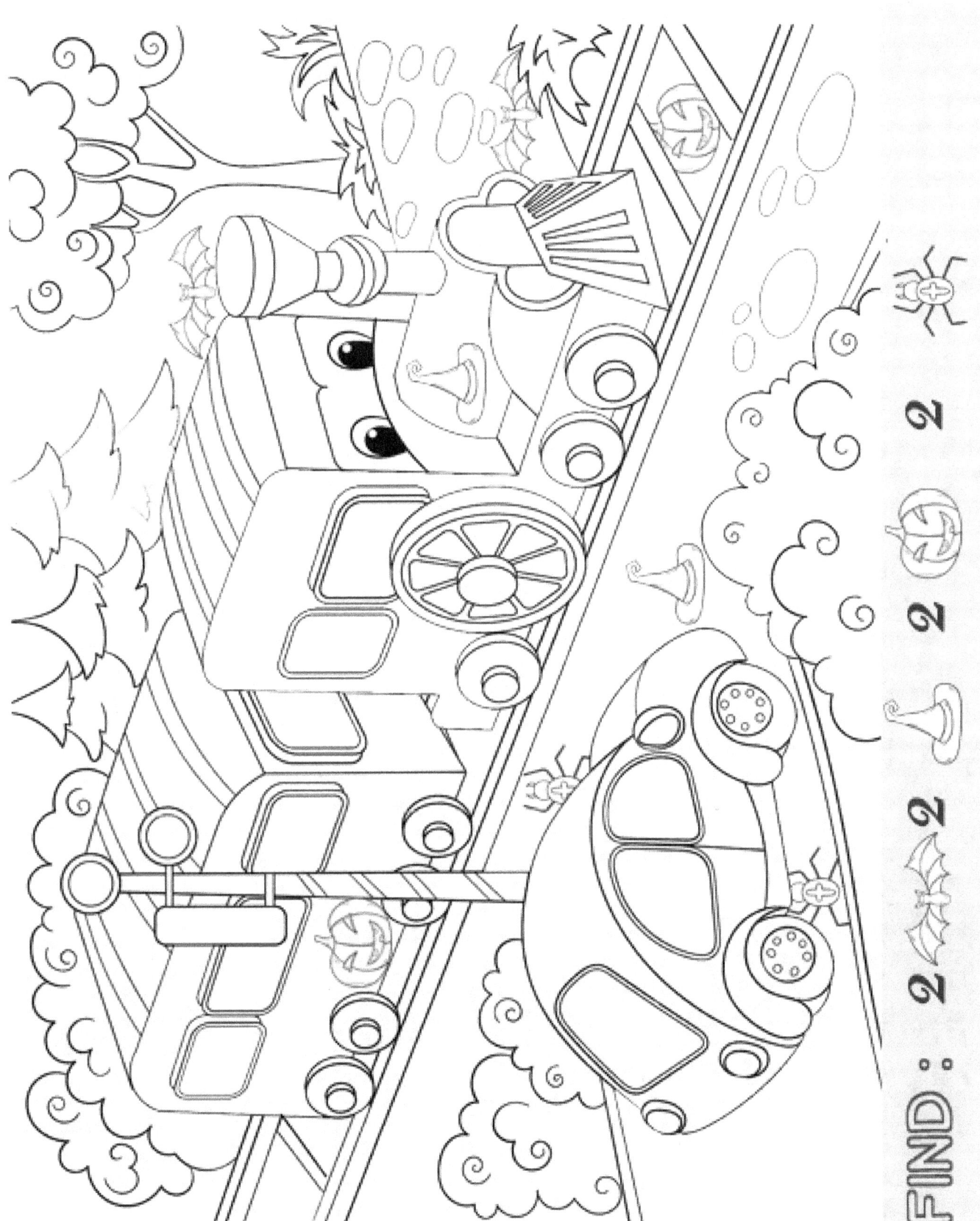

FIND: 2 🕷 2 🦇 2 🍄 2 🍄 2 🍄

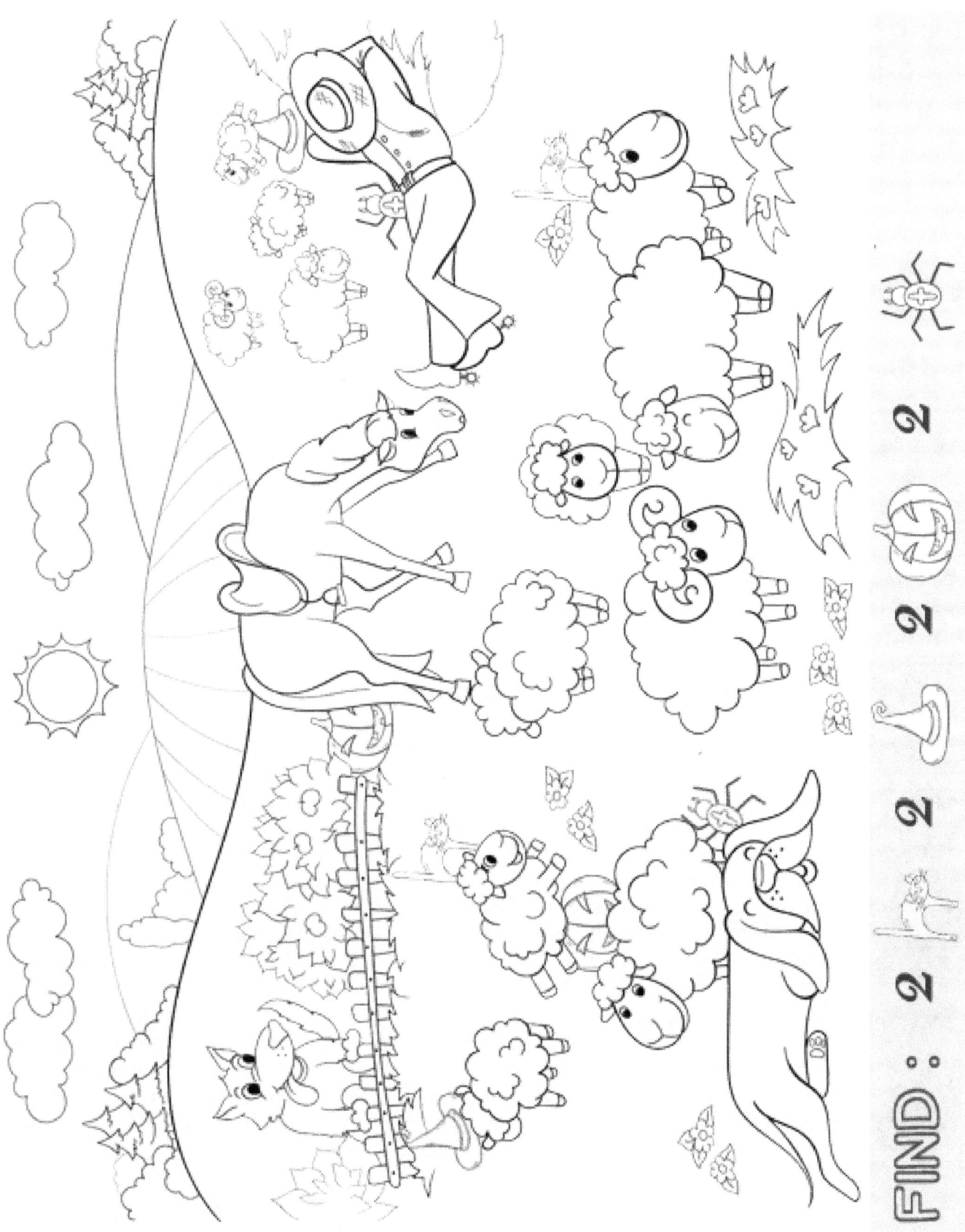

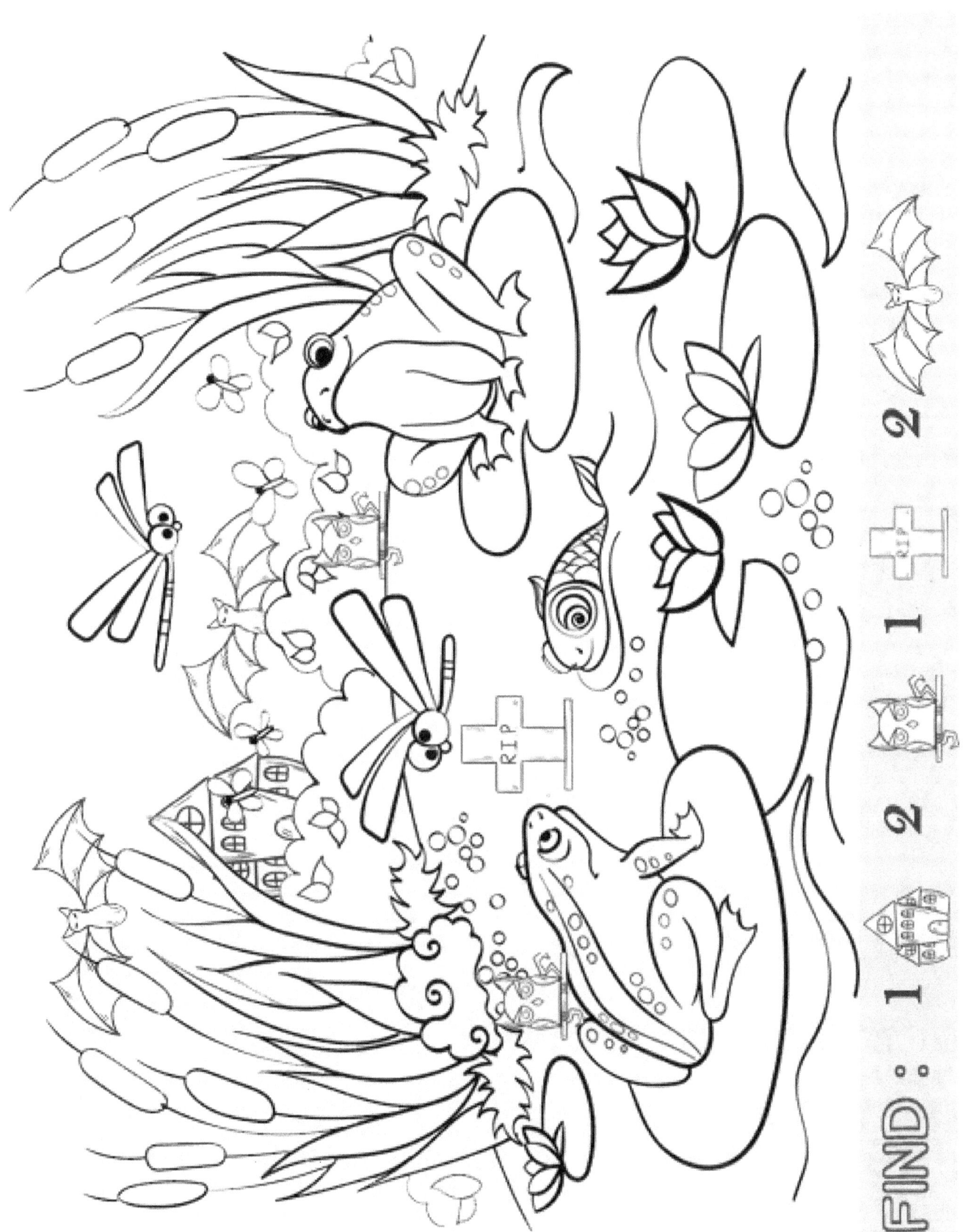

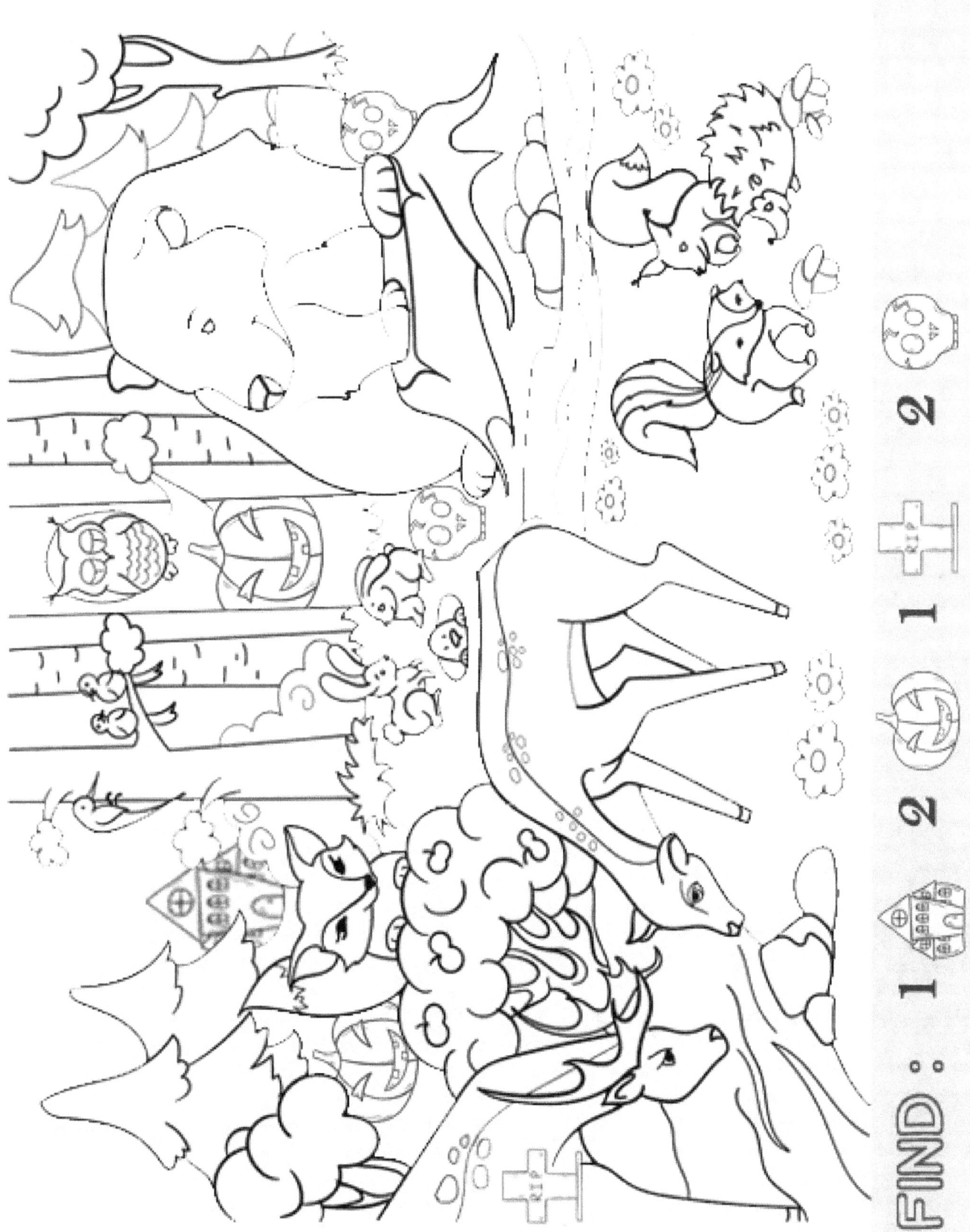

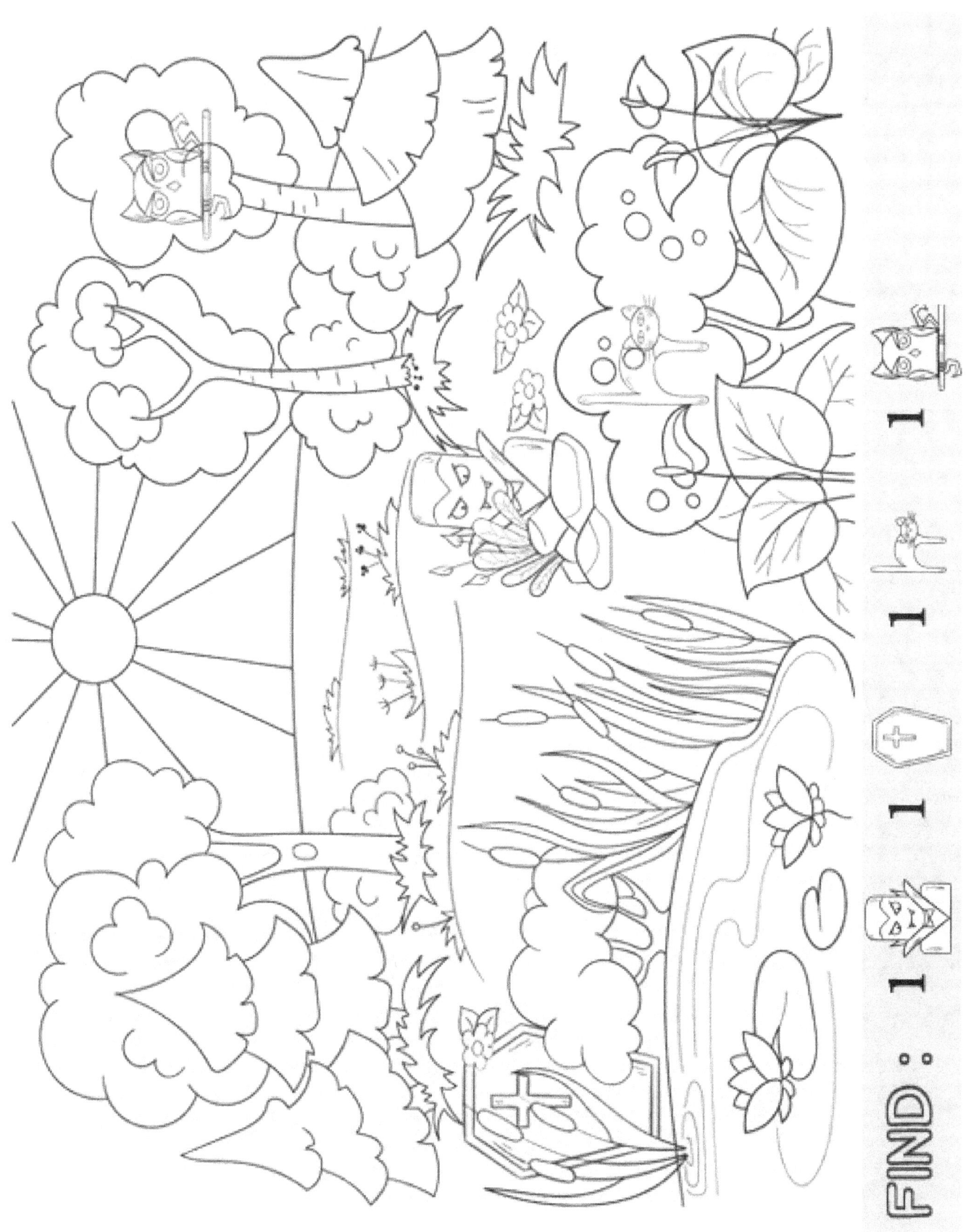

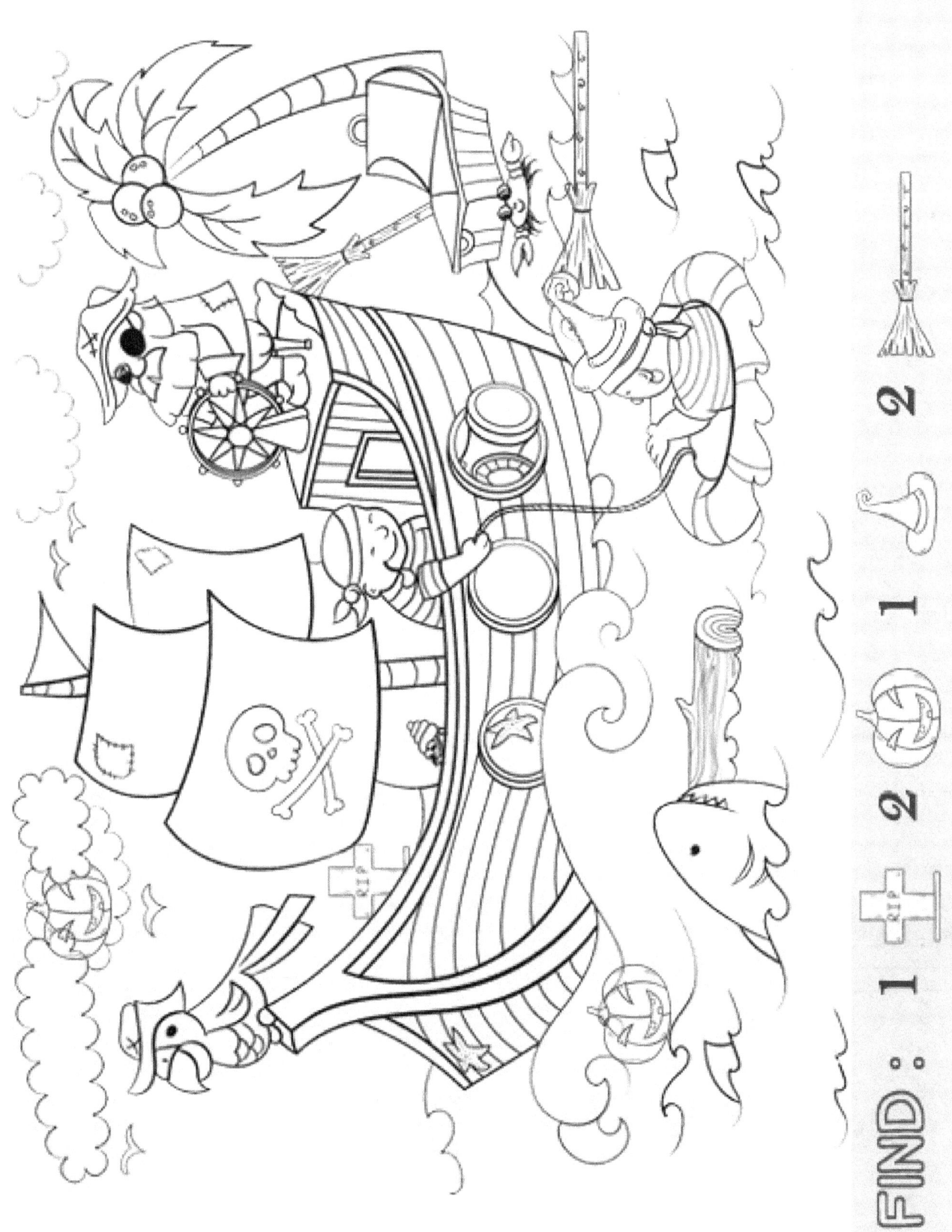

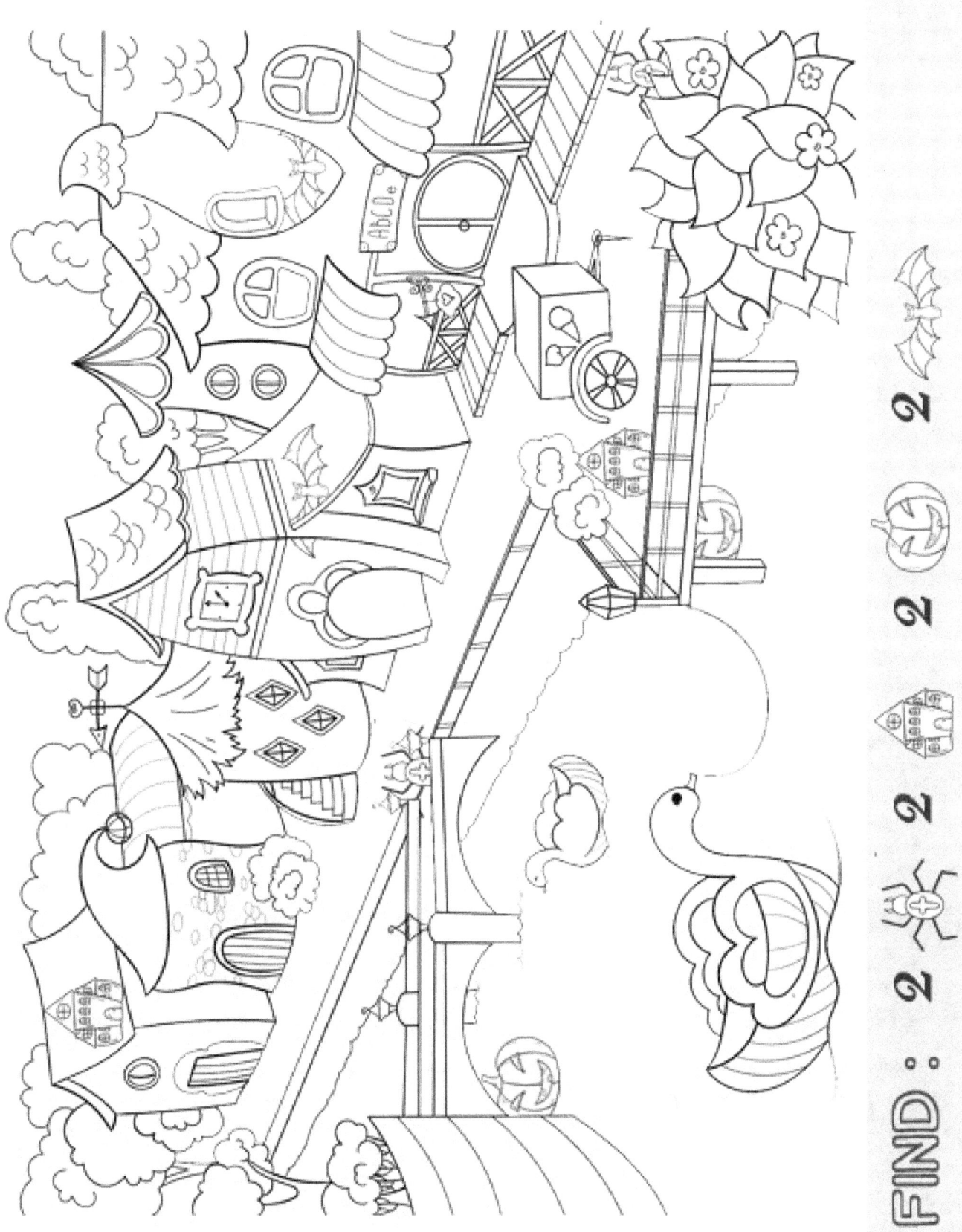

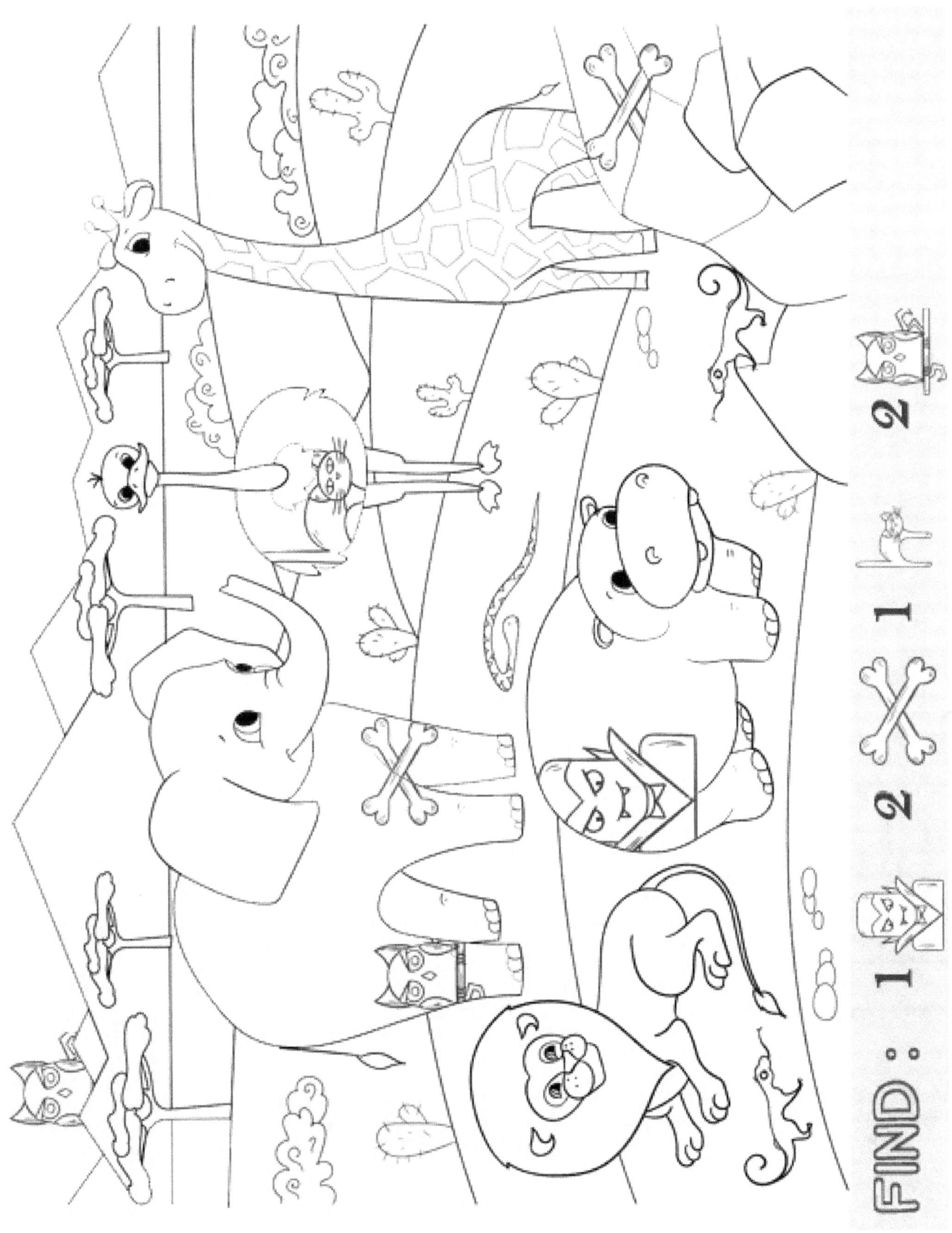

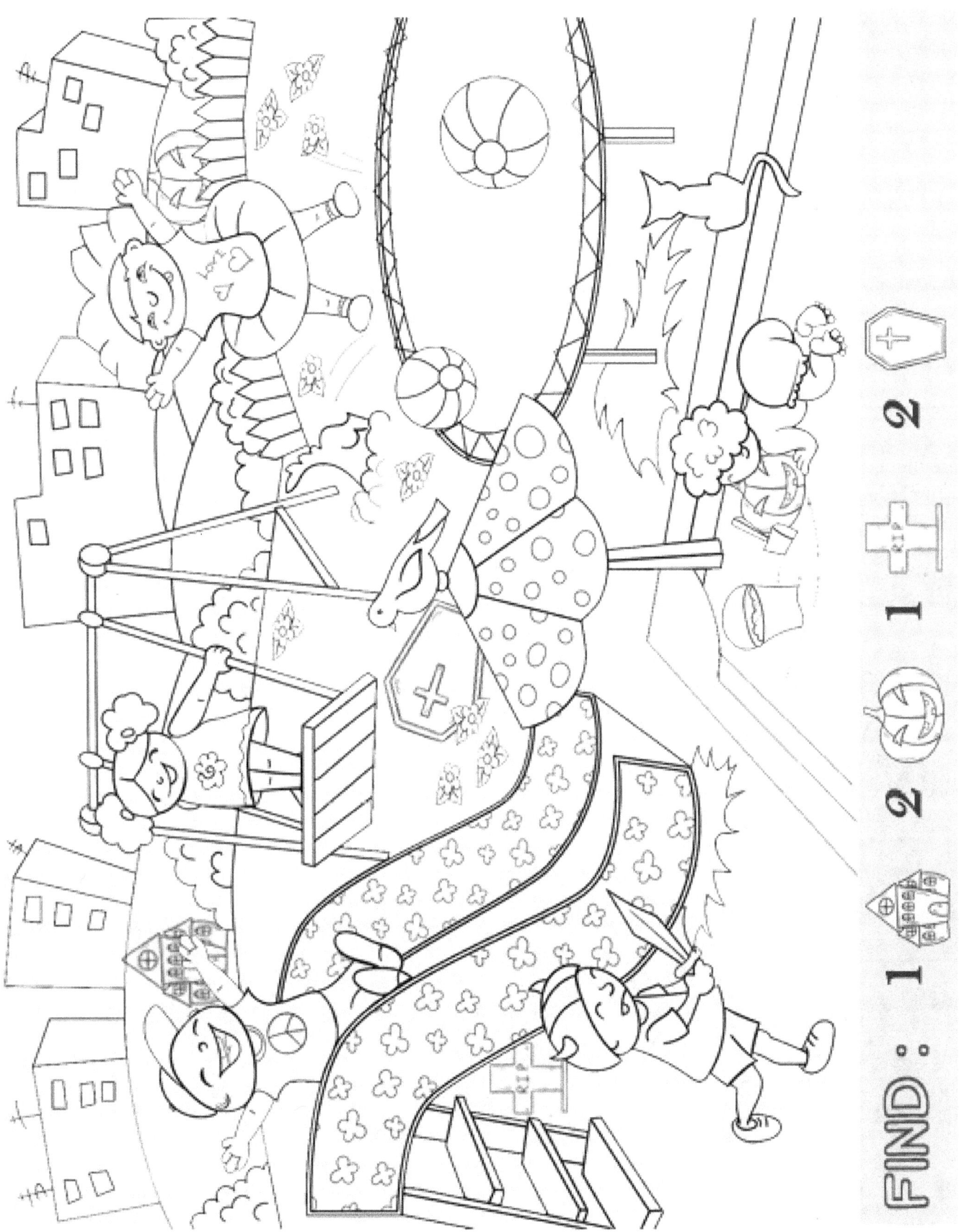

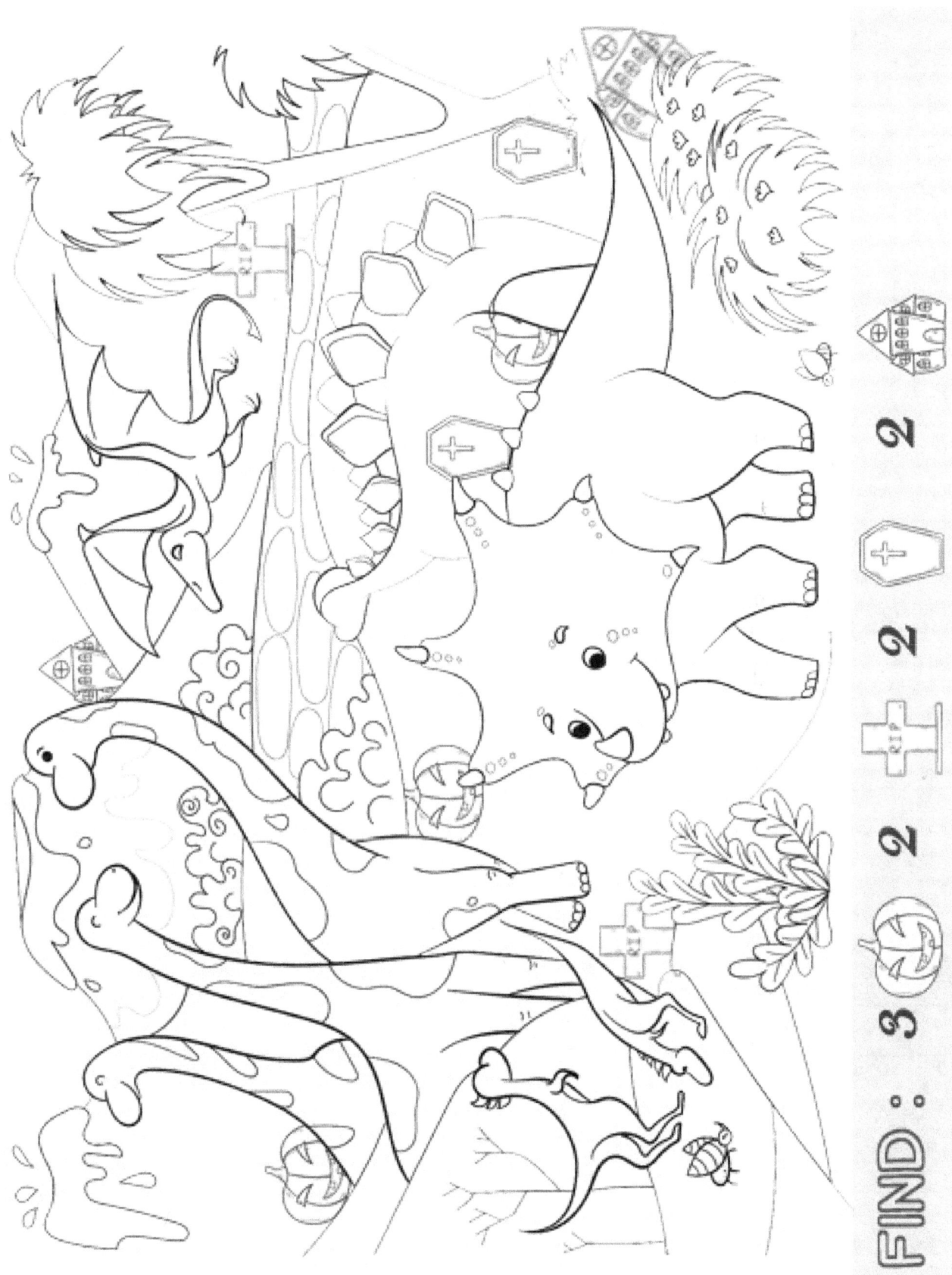

FIND: 3 🦎 2 🌸 2 🏰 2 ✚ 2 🐚 2

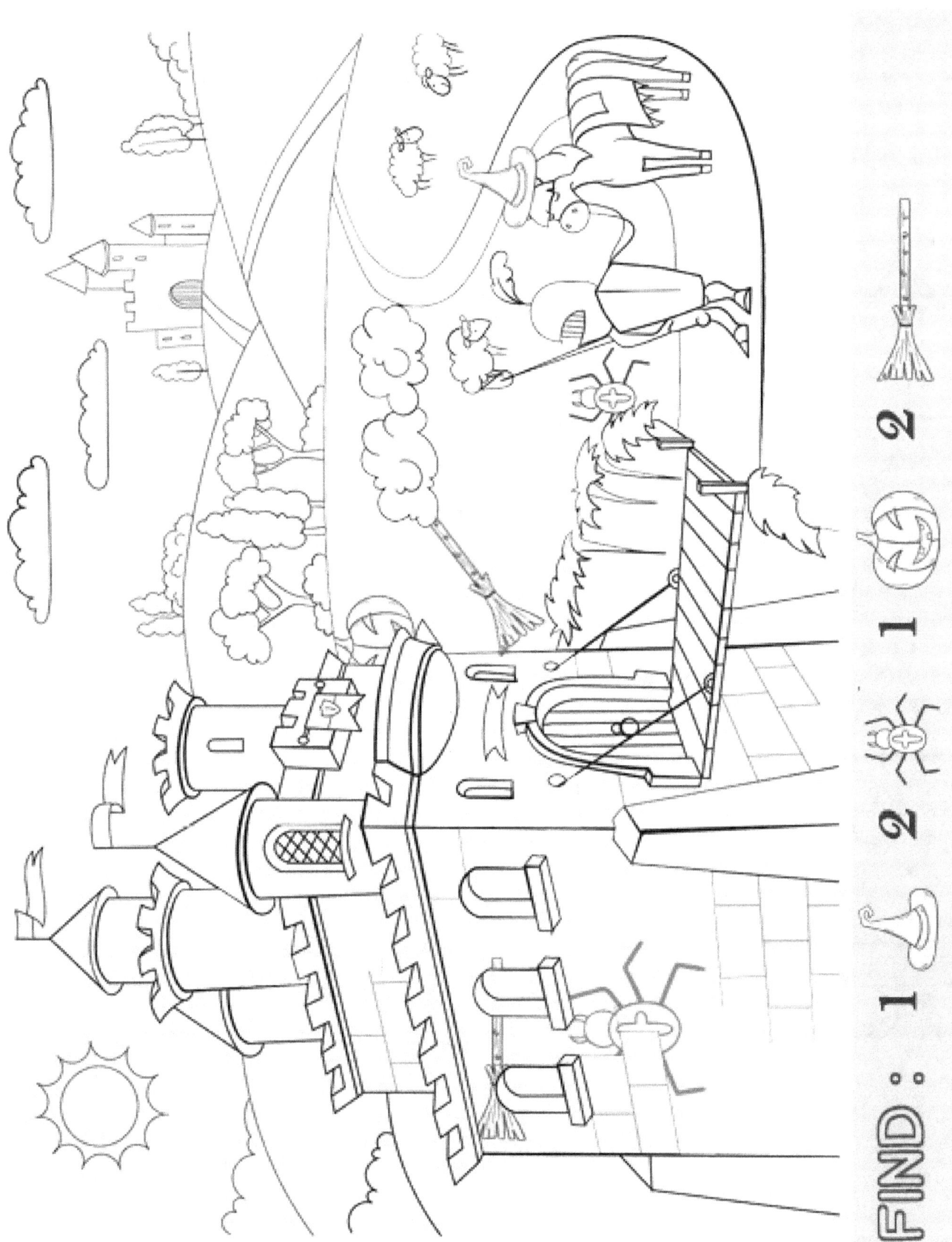

FIND: 1 🍄 2 🕷 1 🎃 2 🧹

HALLOWEEN HIDDEN PICTURES

Coloring Characters For Kids

Copyrighted Material

All rights reserved. No part of this publication may be reproduced, stored in retrieval system, copied in any form or by any means, electronic, mechanical, photocopying, recording or otherwise transmitted without written permission from the publisher.

Kayry Hall